Origins

What's on the Box?

Peter Corey
Character illustrations by Jonatronix

Contents

Switched on	2
How a TV works	4
Early TV	8
TV now	9
Making TV programmes	10
Types of programmes	14
Did you know?	20
TV timeline	22
Glossary	24

OXFORD
UNIVERSITY PRESS

Switched on

Over the last hundred years, the way we **communicate** with each other and how we find out about the world has changed.

Communication then and now

100 years ago	Now
Using our voices	Using our voices
Using our hands and faces	Using our hands and faces
Books and magazines	Books and magazines
Letters and telegrams	Letters and faxes
Carrier pigeon	Radio
	Phone
	Email
	Text messages
	Internet blogs and chatrooms
	Television

Can you think of any other ways we communicate?

Television is now in most of our homes. It has changed the way we communicate.

There are nearly two billion television sets in the world. There are over one hundred different **channels** to choose from. No wonder we sometimes watch too much television.

How many TVs do you have in your house?

The Simpsons are a famous family who love to watch TV.

Have you ever wondered how the pictures get on to your TV? Or how TV programmes are made? We are going to look at how television works.

How a TV works

From the TV station to your home

A television set picks up **video** and **audio** signals sent from a television **station**. The television turns these signals into the pictures we see and the sounds we hear.

3 The TV station **transmits** the signals to a **satellite** high up in space.

2 The signals are sent to a TV channel at a TV station (e.g. BBC, Cartoon Network, Channel 5).

1 The people who make TV programmes record pictures and sounds. These are turned into *digital signals*.

4 The satellite sends the signals back to earth.

5 The signals are sent to satellite dishes, cables, phone lines or aerials attached to people's homes.

6 The signals pass down a wire and into your television.

How does the signal get turned into pictures again?

From signal to screen

Once the digital signals have reached your television, they need to be turned back into pictures and sound.

2 Picture signals are sent as red, green and blue colours.

1 The signals reach a **decoder** in the TV set. The decoder sends the picture signals to pixels on the TV screen.

Fact box

Pixel is short for 'picture element'. A pixel is a single dot on a TV screen. Thousands of pixels make up the picture. The more pixels there are, the better the picture.

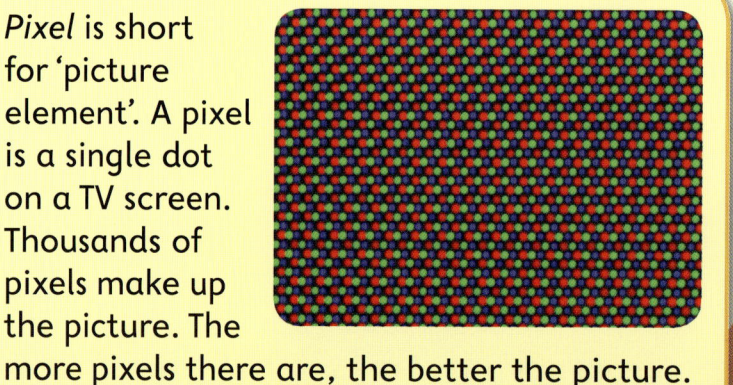

3 As the colours hit the pixels, they light up. This makes the pictures and colours we see on screen.

RED YELLOW GREEN
WHITE
MAGENTA CYAN
BLUE

4 The digital sound signals are added and sent to speakers in the TV set.

5 You can now watch the pictures and hear the sound.

The person who invented television must have been very clever! I wonder who thought all this up?

Early TV

One hundred years ago, there were no televisions. Many scientists and inventors were busy trying to make them.

John Logie Baird got there first! On 27th January, 1926, he showed the first working television in public.

In 1936 there were only 200 television sets in use around the world. TVs were not common in homes until the 1940s. The first television sets were large wooden cabinets with tiny screens.

John Logie Baird and one of his first working televisions. It looks a lot different to TVs today!

TV now

Television has moved on a lot from the early days! Now there are millions of TV sets and we can watch TV programmes on:
- mobile phones
- wrist watches
- handheld computers
- MP3 players.
- the Internet.

We can choose what we want to watch and when. We can choose how we want to see it. There is already lots of choice, but **technology** keeps on changing. What do you think will happen in the future?

Can you think of a cool new way to watch TV?

Making TV programmes

Some television programmes are recorded in a studio. Others are recorded outside a studio. This is called 'on location'.

Location, location

Filming on location is when a programme is made at a real place. This could mean anywhere – inside or outside – on top of a building, in a tunnel, under the sea or up a mountain! Lots of programmes, especially news and sports programmes, are filmed out on location.

At sports events it must be hard to know what is going to happen and where to point the camera!

On set

Sometimes programmes cannot be filmed in a real place. This may be because the story being told happens in a different time or in an imaginary place. A special set may have to be built.

Dr Who is set in an imaginary world so they have to build special sets to create this world.

This is the set of the workhouse from the television drama *Oliver Twist*.

In a studio

Other programmes, such as chat shows and game shows, are filmed in studios. Sometimes audiences are asked in to watch the show.

There are three cameras being used here to film this show. This way, all angles are covered.

What job would you want to do?

Jobs in TV

There are lots of people who will work on a television programme. Here are some of the jobs that you can do:
- **Actor**: acts out the scene
- **Director**: guides the actors through a scene
- **Wardrobe**: looks after the clothes for the actors
- **Camera operator**: records the pictures
- **Grip**: lays the cables and looks after the camera
- **Sound recordist**: records the sound
- **Boom operator**: holds the microphone
- **Gaffer**: is in charge of the lights and electrics
- **Runner**: makes sure everyone has what they want.

After filming

After all the pictures and sound have been recorded, they have to be put together in the right order to make a programme. Sometimes special effects need to be added. Special effects are used to alter the recorded pictures by adding, removing or changing the way people and things look. This is often done with the help of computers. An *editor* will put all the different parts together with the help of the director.

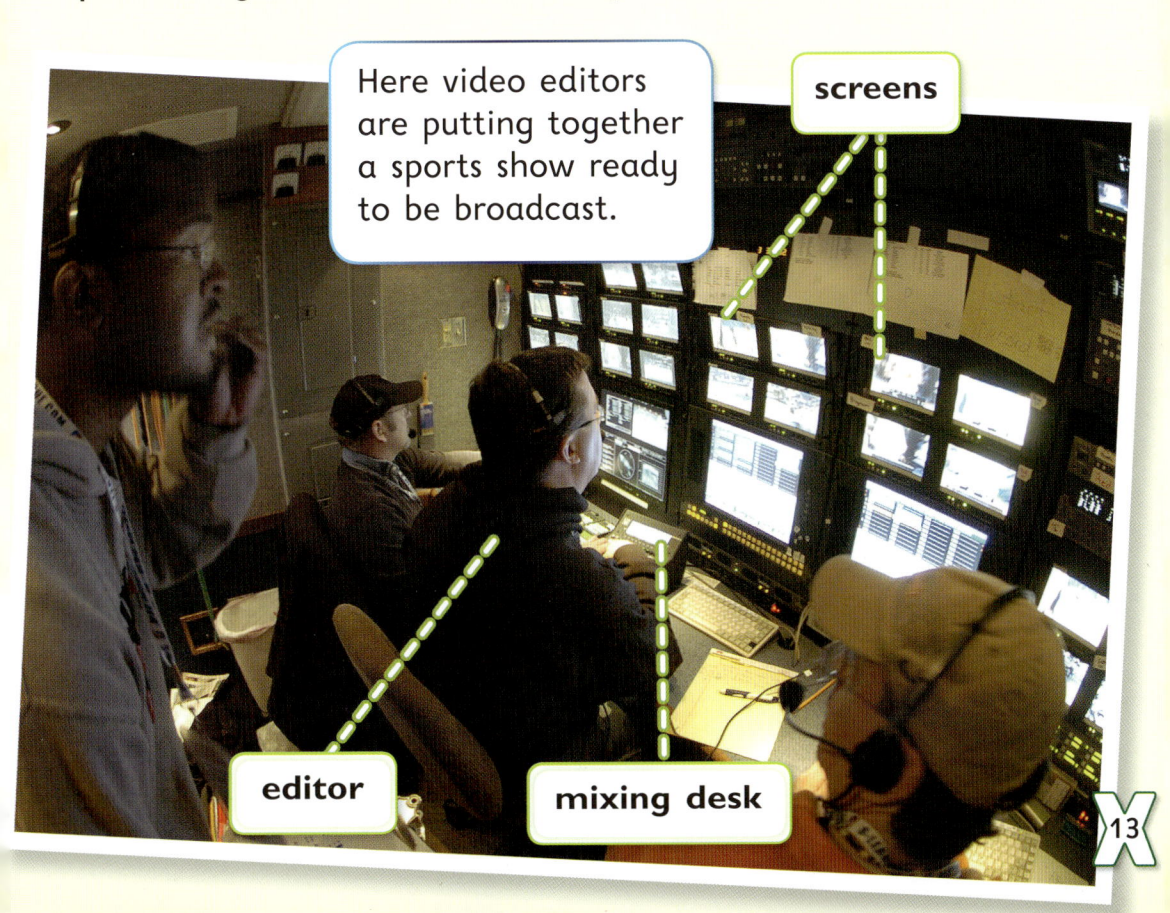

Here video editors are putting together a sports show ready to be broadcast.

screens

editor

mixing desk

Types of programmes

The news

TV can help us find out what is going on in the world. It can communicate the news as soon as it happens, even if it happens on the other side of the world.

These villagers in Africa are talking to a **reporter**.

The news is shown at regular intervals on many TV channels.

How do you think people heard about the news before there were TVs?

On 21st July 1969, Neil Armstrong became the first man to walk on the moon. 600 million people around the world watched this happen on television.

In 2001, Ellen MacArthur became the youngest person and the fastest woman to sail round the world on her own. News programmes across the world reported on her progress as she sailed into the record books.

What important news stories have you seen on TV?

Our world

A hundred years ago, most people did not know very much about our world. People read about far-off places in books. Now, TV can communicate sights and sounds from around the world to everyone.

We can watch volcanoes erupt from the safety of our homes. We can see far-off countries without going anywhere. We can get close to **endangered** animals in their natural habitats. Explorers and **naturalists** use television to share their knowledge of the world.

One of the most famous naturalists is Sir David Attenborough. For more than 50 years he has been filming our planet and its wildlife and sharing his knowledge and his experience. His TV programmes have helped us to know more about our planet and how precious it is.

I want to be like David Attenborough when I grow up. Who do you want to be like?

David Attenborough with a rare golden eagle.

Entertainment

Television is not just for watching the news and finding out about the world. There are programmes to entertain us, too. There are music and sport programmes, soaps, cartoons, quiz shows, films, travel shows, comedy and drama programmes.

The quiz show *The Weakest Link* is presented by Anne Robinson. It has been so popular that it is now shown in 75 countries around the world!

There are lots of special interest channels, too:
- Music channels
- History channels
- Movie channels
- Shopping channels
- Cartoon channels

What's your favourite type of TV programme?

Scooby Doo was a cartoon first shown in 1969 and is still popular today.

SpongeBob Squarepants was created by Steve Hillenburg. He came up with the idea because he used to be a marine biologist (which means that he studied life under the sea).

Did you know?

> How much time do you spend watching TV?

The first UK TV broadcast was made on 20th August, 1929.

We spend an average of 28 hours a week watching TV – that's *four hours a day*! Boys generally watch more TV than girls.

Blue Peter is the longest-running children's TV programme in the world. It started in 1958 and is still running today.

This is Gethin Jones. He was a *Blue Peter* presenter from 2005–2008.

Sesame Street is the most widely viewed children's series in the world. It started in 1969 and has won over 100 awards!

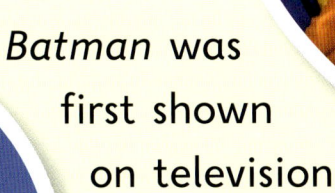

Batman was first shown on television in 1966. He started life in a comic in 1939.

The Simpsons has been shown in more than 90 countries. It is the longest running cartoon show.

TV timeline

1900   The word 'television' is used for the first time.

1925   A Scotsman called John Logie Baird transmits the first television image.

1926   John Logie Baird shows television working in public.

1930   There are just 200 TV sets in the world.

1951 The first colour TVs go on sale.

1956 The TV remote control is invented.

1969 TV is broadcast from the moon!

Now we can watch TV anywhere – amazing!

2009 There are now 2 billion TV sets in the world!

Glossary

audio   sound

channel   a service or station that transmits programmes

communicate   talking or writing to someone

decoder   a device that turns digital signals back into pictures and sound

endangered   in danger of dying out

naturalist   someone who studies nature

reporter   someone who writes about something that has happened

satellite   a spacecraft that moves around the Earth and sends signals down to it

technology   studying machines and how things work

station   a building that transmits programmes

transmit   to send out signals for TV and radio programmes

video   relating to recording and reproducing pictures